Livin' Under Goldie's Rules

SAM PEMBERTON

Publishing Coordinator – Sharon Kizziah-Holmes
Cover Design – Sharon Kizziah-Holmes

Paperback-Press
an imprint of A & S Publishing
Paperback Press, LLC.

ISBN -13: 978-1-956806-72-4

DEDICATION

This book is dedicated to my sister Mattie Jo
Pemberton Wilson. She was 11 years older than me
and she was a positive influence on her little
brother. She taught me a lot of things from tying my
shoes to combing my hair. Things Goldie didn't
have time for Mattie Jo took care of it. She was
always able to provide encouragement and love I
needed.

Between the two of them they prove the old
adage that the hand that rocks the cradle rules the
world. I still live by Goldie's rules and Mattie Jo's
encouragement.

ACKNOWLEDGMENTS

There are three ladies I can't thank enough.

First and foremost, my wife Pat. Thank you being my sidekick all these years. We make a good team. I'd also like to thank you for helping find last minute mistakes in my book. You're the only proofreader I absolutely love.

Nancy Dailey, what a blessing you've been. Thank you for putting all the pieces of my book together. You take editing to the next level. I not sure you know how much I appreciate you for your hours of hard work to make everything flow the way it's supposed to.

Last but definitely not least, kudos to my publishing coordinator Sharon Kizziah-Holmes of Paperback Press. Sharon, without your expertise and advice, I don't think this book would have come to fruition. Thank you for sending me to Nancy, thank you for putting together the cover of Living Under Goldie's Rules and just for being you. I'm grateful I found you and your company to make my publishing dream come true.

PREFACE

The idea for writing *Livin' Under Goldie's Rules* came about over the years when every time I started to make a decision, or comment, I would think of what she might say. My mother's influence from what I believe to what I do is constant. She taught me hard work, she taught me to work hard. There's a difference between working hard and being willing to accept that sometimes we have to do a hard task.

This book is her story of adjustment to changes in life. Her pursuit of independence. The problems with isolation and trying to raise her family. I review how she dealt with everything she had to face. I loved writing it because I tell *my* story at the same time. I show the connection of a mother's love for her youngest child and the benefits I received from being that child.

I also relate to special treatment I received from one person in particular; My sister Mattie Joe, who became my second mother.

Recently I joined Facebook where I've shared a lot of philosophy. I always say 'it's one of Goldie's rules'. There are many rules and this story is an attempt to show how her life, and her ideas, continue through those who called her mom or just Goldie.

As you read, hopefully you'll realize how our thinking is implanted from the day we are born. Enjoy the story, and relate to the life *you* have enjoyed.

CHAPTER 1

-❦•❦-

West of where the Highway 14 bridge crosses Big Creek now, stood the original log house of the Sutterfield homestead. Goldie Emmaline was born there on October 27, 1913, the fifth child of Henry and Stacy Rose Sutterfield.

The house, built in the early 1800s, originally had two big log rooms, but had been added on to by the time Goldie was born. Some houses like this had dirt floors, but the floors in this log house had been hewn by hand, and joined in place, creating a solid wood floor. Goldie always talked about the status symbol of not being raised on a dirt floor.

The house was set in a cedar glade with a spring flowing out of the limestone hill not very many yards away. The cluster of farm buildings was built away from the spring to keep from polluting the water used for the house. The hog pen and hog house were the greatest distance from the spring.

This area of the Ozark Mountains, in the northeastern part of Searcy County, Arkansas, was beautiful with its perfectly clear streams and an abundance of wild game. The hills are flint stone that had formed on top of the clay-based mountains, which had eroded away leaving the rocks exposed. Geologically this is part of the Mississippi dome with part of the farmland formed from the sediment that ran off of the hills during the centuries prior to any settlers.

Goldie's father, and his father before him, had farmed the homestead. They earned their living by growing their food and using the methods of canning vegetables, drying fruits, and curing meat that had existed for years. They were adept at harvesting game, and drying the hides for sale or to use to create articles of clothing.

The only means of transportation at the time was horse-drawn buggies and wagons. You could own the fanciest buggy in the neighborhood, but you were limited to traveling along the creeks and following the various wagon trails that had been cut out and maintained for horse-drawn transportation. 1913 was several years before automobiles began to appear in the area. When automobiles did come, there was still nothing more than those wagon trails, making it basically impossible to use cars there.

The homestead had been built close to water. While there was a stream flowing constantly in the creek below, the house had to be built away from that to avoid flooding.

Goldie's family at Big Creek where she was born.
Front row: Goldie's father Henry Sutterfield, her brother
Noble and her mother Stacy.
Back row: Goldie's sister Oakla, Goldie then her sisters Gertie
and Ethel.

Farming was done in the fertile little patch of
land on top of the bluffs, called bench land. Along
the creeks there were little fertile patches of land
referred to as bottoms. Goldie's grandfather had
chosen the spot above Big Creek, which was
bounded by Hickory Hollow on the north, a small

3

spring-fed stream and a couple of other large hollows that made their junction with Big Creek in the immediate area. While they cleared all the land they intended to farm, they left the other cedar glades alone to provide shelter for animals, and also as a windbreak during winter. Since the time the settlers had arrived, they developed a system of trails to get from one homestead to the other. All the families knew the shortest route to go see their neighbor.

Goldie grew up walking up to 2 ½ miles to visit the relative that lived the farthest away. She related many stories of walking those trails and visiting with her grandmother and grandfather Rose who still operated a gristmill on Cedar Creek to the south and east.

Her education consisted of a few months of school during the summer after the crops were laid by. She went to school at the Cedar Grove schoolhouse located on the eastern side of Big Creek, less than a mile from her house. A good number of students walked from all directions to arrive at the one room school building. It is amazing how well these people learned to read and write and also how to do arithmetic. This was the time when "school" referred to learning the 3Rs; Reading, 'Riting, and 'Rithmatic.

Reading included the art of spelling, while writing involved the application of putting what they had learned on paper.

Goldie's early childhood was influenced by the people that lived in and around the homestead, all within walking distance. She lived all her life in that one spot until she married Arvil Pemberton on July 30, 1929. Goldie was 16 years old, Arvil was 18. They moved into one of the tenant farm houses for a few years. They left Big Creek and moved to Leslie, Arkansas, where Arvil worked in the stave mill business. After three or four years they returned to Big Creek. Their first child, Ida, was born on Big Creek. Mattie Jo was born in Leslie, Jim was born after they returned to the Sutterfield homestead. Nell was born just south and east of the Big Creek bridge where Goldie grew up.

In the 1930s a large number of people deserted their homesteads and moved to California or other parts West. Goldie and Arvil also moved with their children, but they only moved about three and a half miles. They bought the farm on Bratton Creek.

Pemberton family taken on Bratton Creek.
Front row: Sam, Nell, Jim.
Back row: Ida, mom Goldie, dad Arvel, Mattie.

Taken in front of the house on Bratton Creek where Sam was born. Sam, his dad Arvel and Nell.

This is where I met Goldie. I was born October 21, 1944. Goldie was my mother. Like my mother, I was the fifth child in the family. My two older sisters were 12 and 13 years older than me. My brother was seven years older, and my youngest sister was a year and a half older.

About the time I was born, Grandpa and Granny Sutterfield moved to Big Flat. That meant my mom's family was no longer close enough to share their day-to-day lives together. Another consequence of this was that she had trouble adjusting to the move to Bratton, away from the homestead. It was very traumatic for her.

When I was a kid my parents spent a great deal of their time reminiscing about their school at Cedar Grove. Mom shared some of the ways they used to learn. For example, when she learned her ABCs, she learned them by reciting, "A is for apple, B bit it, C cut it, D divided it," and so on. The thing I remember the most about Mom's way of learning things, and my favorite, was how she taught me to spell "geography." **G**eorge **E**lliott's Old **G**oose **R**an **A P**ig **H**ome **Y**esterday. That was well before I started school.

I remember when I was four sitting in her lap watching the sun go down as darkness came up the hollow and the sun tipped the tops of the mountains as it set. Mom explained how it worked, that the world was round and the sun was going west as the Earth rotated east. Now think about Goldie trying to explain that to a child four years old.

After several times of her telling me how it worked as we watched the sun go down, I felt confident enough to try to explain it to my new friend, Fred Watts. That may be where my reputation was ruined about being a know-it-all for a young man.

When all the other kids had started school, it was just Mom and me during the day. Some of my favorite times was digging a can of worms and going fishing in the little holes of water on Bratton Creek. She was a good fisherman, and later in life one of her favorite things was to take our youngest daughter, Sherri, with her to the farm on Bear Creek and fish in much the same way she and I had fished when I was Sherri's age. She had insisted that I learn to put the worm on my hook myself, and I did. Sherri had to do the same thing when she went with Mom. I remember the phone call when Mom told me, "Sherri is just like you were when you were a kid. It didn't bother her a bit to put that worm on that hook."

Goldie and I made day trips, walking from the homestead down to Bratton Creek. When we were ready to cross the creek, it was time to decide where we were going to go. We could go up the hollow all the way to the Watts farm, or we could turn and climb the bluff along the trail and go to her cousins'. Goldie made the decisions where we went. I loved going to Fred's, but she loved to go see her cousins. If we climbed the bluff and took that trail, the first house we would come to was Barry and Nellie's house. When we got close enough, we would hear their dogs start barking. Mom was acquainted well enough that when she yelled, "Shut up!" the dogs would stop barking. And that was an instruction that became a part of Goldie's rules. When she said, "Shut up!" that's what you did.

We had a black dog, whose name would not be politically correct today, that followed us wherever we went. I don't remember him ever fighting with these dogs. Evidently, they had worked that out earlier.

Goldie was loud. When she got close, the people would come out, regardless of whose house we were going to, and the visiting began before we ever made it to their house. It was usually answering questions about what we were doing, why we were coming, and a list of answers that was given out by the time we got there.

When we arrived, no matter the time of day, we were offered food. There was something special about each house and the food they would have. Barry and Nellie would always have some kind of wild game they had cooked. I don't remember what it was, I just remember Goldie had some rules about some of the stuff she would not eat.

I remember we always ate with Cordy Watts and Fred. The Watts family had more people eat with them than anyone I van ever remember. Oscar operated a blacksmith shop and would put shoes on horses and mules. He sharpened all kinds of farm tool, plus they had a gristmill for grinding corn.

Sometimes we ate with Mom's cousins, Barry, or Theodore Sutterfield. Theodore was Mom's first cousin, and he was married to my dad's sister, Zelma, a Pemberton. Uncle Theodore was the first person I ever saw that baked sweet potatoes from his garden. He called them "fart roots." Of course, I remembered that! To this day, Mom's instructions were always that Theodore and Zelma's family was special because "we were a lot akin to those folks."

The typical family arrived from Tennessee and settled along with their neighbors that had made the trip to Arkansas with them. Relationships to this day are based on those original settlers that came together. I have prejudices that Mom instilled in me that I spent a lifetime trying to get rid of, that go back to grudges between families that came to Arkansas about the same time. Mom's instructions on who I could associate with stuck with me through the years.

If somebody had stolen a garden hoe a hundred years earlier, and that family had moved and settled five miles away, it was still off limits according to Goldie to ever associate with those folks.

A lot of people have tried to write this period of

history as a very special time when everybody loved everybody and there was no problems or prejudices. Goldie loved ninety per cent of the folks, but the ten per cent she couldn't stand, she made it clear.

Goldie's rules included a lot of sayings. "Plant a pumpkin, you get a pumpkin." "If that much is bad, they're bad to the core." I don't know whether this is good or bad. We live in a day right now when there is probably nothing different than it's ever been, but the things I learned early seem to be stuck in place.

When we were ready to go home from visiting the neighbors, if they gave us something to take with us, we had to make sure it wasn't too heavy to carry all the way back home. Then when we got home, we had to start the evening chores. Most of the time, Dad would be back from wherever he was working, the bigger kids would be back, and it became a family project for all of us to do our chores.

I don't know when I actually got things assigned to me to do as my share of the chores. I think the first, though, that I got from Goldie regarding chores was to make sure that the wood box by the cookstove was full. The wood was split in smaller strips, and there was usually dried oak laying in a pile out in the chip yard by all the other wood. I don't know how many I could carry, but I would carry an armload up the back steps and through the kitchen to the box that set by the stove.

The problem I usually ran into was stepping in the mud, dropping bark and chips as I made my way through the kitchen, and putting green wood on top.

'Til this day I think my work ethic was developed by Goldie. She tolerated failure. I had no trouble as long as I didn't do something repeatedly. She made every effort to give me a fair chance, but if then I didn't get it right, the instructions changed to corporal punishment. I'm not saying she beat me every day, I'm sure she didn't, but the back of her hand, and a little switch applied to the backside was the best teaching method of the day.

The place where I lived was where the groves widened out enough to build a house. There was a ledge above the house that I thought was tall, and it was an excellent place to play. I took my girls over there to show them where I grew up my first five years, and I was amazed when I got there. The little bluff behind the house that I thought was tall was scarcely knee high to me as an adult. I remembered a hole in the bluff that I would put things in, and I thought it was huge, but it was hardly bigger than my fist.

The Bratton farm was no different than any other homestead. A spring supplied the water for the house. There was a spring box that sat in the flow of the spring and contained the milk, butter, and everything else that had to be kept cool. The box was designed with a tight lid, and had shelves inside above the waterline. The items that needed to be kept cool but dry, were stored at this level. The milk and things that needed to be colder were on a shelf low enough to be about half underwater. Drinking water was dipped out above the spring box.

Rather than carry water from the spring to do laundry, we would take the laundry to the spring.

There was a kettle for heating water in an area some distance below the spring. I remember the problem Mom would have getting the water just the right temperature for washing clothes. If it was too hot, she would add cold water from the spring. If it wasn't hot enough, she would add wood to the fire.

The washing was done on an old-style rub board that extended down into the water in a tub. The clothes were pulled up and rubbed on the corrugated section of the washboard. Can you imagine a woman bending over a tub full of water, pulling out clothes and scrubbing them until she thought they were clean? The dirtiest clothes were saved until last. Mom placed them in the kettle and boiled them before she scrubbed them on the washboard.

It seemed like it was a long way to the spring to do laundry, but in reality, it was scarcely more than 100 yards.

Going to the spring had a lot of rules. One was that I was never to go near the drinking water or the box where we kept the milk and butter. One day, with Mom busy over the rub board washing clothes, I decided to take a whiz into the spring. I did this above where the milk and butter were in the box. There is no lapse in memory about the instructions Goldie gave me accompanied with a treatment from a switch. Trust me, I have never gone by the spring and took a leak again. I remember that rule every time I see spring water running out of a hill.

The trail to the spring was no different than the other trails we followed around the farm. We had to stay in the trail to avoid ticks and chiggers. We also had to watch for snakes. On one of our trips back from the spring we encountered a huge snake ready to do battle. Mom got a stick and started the battle. I can't accurately describe this because she told me to get back. I had no trouble running back toward the spring. I stayed away until she told me it was okay. Her instructions were "if you ever see one of those things again, don't start a fight with it."

She didn't have to worry.

She burned out on living on Bratton and was ready to leave the primitive homestead. Dad loved having a farm in the middle of the woods. The farm had decent land and adequate water. It was comparable to living in today's cabins that are hunting camps. Dad did some trapping for hides, and always either hunted or fished, claiming it was for food. And it was.

Isolation was a problem for Goldie. There were old farmsteads that people deserted in the 30s during the Depression. During World War II other people moved to where there were good jobs. The last close neighbors we had were Earl and Velma Wallace. They lived in a tenant farm that Dad owned about a half-mile from us. Before them, Ben and Bama Seton had lived there. But Earl and Velma moved to Idaho. That left us alone on Bratton with Jim and Nell walking to Harriet to school, while Ida and Mattie Jo stayed with Granny in Big Flat to go to high school.

A child of five is too young to have an opinion. But it seems to me like Goldie would not shut up about moving away from Bratton. She agreed that Dad could keep the farm, but she also said that I was not going to walk to school across that dark hollow like Nell and Jim were having to do.

Part of Mom's values were set by things she learned from her extended family along the banks of Big Creek and Cedar Creek. The other part she learned in the old school building, which also served as the church for the community. School met during the summer, and usually that was the time that a revival was held by some traveling minister. This was before Sunday school and typical church services had started. They were not very denominational. Most people were Baptist. Pentecostal people hadn't yet arrived in the area.

My earliest memories include instructions on how to stay out of the seed ticks, avoid snakes, and run errands to and from the farm buildings. Goldie's instructions were always the rules I had to live by. "Don't break the eggs, make sure you don't bring in the nest egg, and only get what you can carry. Don't step in anything in the barnyard and track it into the house, don't pet the dogs and handle the cats while you're carrying in food. Make sure you stay where I can call you if I need to. Don't ever leave the yard unless you tell me why."

I was allowed to go as far as the hog pen after the hogs were fed, and I could sit on the bluff, which was actually just a ledge above the pen, and watch the hogs. One time I got too close, and slid off the ledge into the pen with the hogs.

I can't actually say I remember this. I heard the story so much I think I remember being in the pen with the hogs. I remember being so scared of the sows as they got closer to me. I know I yelled. Goldie's description was, "That kid gave out with the loudest scream I ever heard!"

Goldie never had to tell me again how far away to stay from the hogs.

CHAPTER 2

-ᴥ•ᴥ-

The J. W. Davis farm was in the Big Flat school district, and the school bus ran on Highway 14 to Big Flat through his property. J. W. was Mom's nephew, the son of Mom's sister, Oakley. Mom talked to J. W., and he agreed to let us have a spot of land to build a house. Dad did not want to do this at all. Mom made it clear that J. W. had agreed to give us the spot of land, and he was going to build her a house. Dad continually pointed out how hard it would be to move to a place that didn't have water. He kept saying, "No water, no buildings, just a dry ridge."

There is a picture of Dad, Blaine, Jim, and me standing in the woods in front of that house. It was taken shortly after we moved there. There is nothing but trees and rocks around the house. It is easy to understand Dad's opinion of how desolate that place was compared to a homestead that had a building of every kind you would ever need.

Sam's dad Arvel, brother Jim, brother-in-law Blane Watts
and Sam

First picture taken after the move to the road in 1950.
Front row: Nell, Sam
Back row: Jim, Ida, Goldie, Arvel, Mattie.

The house was located about a mile and a half east of the Hickory Hollow Baptist Church and the Firestone's store at Harriet. There was another store at Harriet across the street from Firestone's. This was the junction of Highway 27 that went to Yellville and Highway 14 that went to Big Flat. In September, 1950, the house was finished. We moved.

It took several years to establish everything and we still walked back and forth to Bratton. There were times you couldn't take a truck because the road flooded. All the reasons that Goldie wanted to leave Bratton were the things that made it hard to take care of the farm.

She never regretted leaving.

Goldie took her chickens, the ones she was able to catch, and moved to a place she hated almost as bad as Bratton. One thing I will say for my mother is that she would adjust really quickly to a new situation if people would listen and correct the problems she wanted fixed. I have been accused of not having a lot of patience when I am trying to get something done. Goldie's rule was, "If you can identify a problem, eliminate it."

The transition period from Bratton to the highway was the most traumatic time I remember in my early years. Mom had won. She had a new house and was close to her nephew. I was closer to Fred. Plus, Dad's brother Ollie lived less than 300 yards from us. Dad was not happy.

Arvel and Goldie standing by the house built on the road.

The Pemberton family at the house on the road.
Front row, kneeling: Nell, Mattie, Sam.
Back row: Arvel, Goldie, Ida, Jim.

I remember the biggest problem was to keep enough water to do laundry and to stay clean. There was an immediate effort to dig a cistern to catch rainwater from the roof, which was the system most houses along dry ridges had. If this move had not been Goldie's idea, we would've been back on Bratton in less than two weeks.

One thing about Goldie's rules, when you make a decision, you're stuck. It was up to us to figure this out. Until the cistern was dug, we got water barrels, and put up guttering to fill them with rainwater. We had a Dozier dig a small pond for water for the cow. The only animals we brought from Bratton were the chickens, for eggs, and one cow, for milk. Dad immediately began building a small barn for the cow and for hay, and a chicken lot for Mom's chickens because they were dying in the road, run over by cars.

Mom began to settle in. I'm not sure how long this all took because I had to start school at Big Flat immediately when we moved. Mom rode the bus with me and Fred that first day. She sat between us as we rode that bus some nine miles or better to school. I was scared to death. I had never been out on my own other than going to church or visiting with family. Mom took us in the school and we were introduced to our teacher, Miss Mae Adams. One of the first people we saw was my cousin, Harold Sutterfield. Fred and I began to relax because we now were three guys in the first grade together. While the school seemed big with all ages of kids, including high school seniors, we began to settle in. Mom told the teacher that if Fred or I either one gave her a problem to let her know. Just another one of Goldie's rules.

School was a whole new experience, but Fred and I both fell in love with it.

I can't say when I met Fred, but he was my lifelong friend. When we moved up to the road, it put me very close to Fred's house. I don't know how to compare us to anyone. When we started to school the family compared us to Tom Sawyer and Huck Finn. With Blaine and Ida being married, our families were tied together. Fred had six brothers and three sisters; he was next to the youngest. I came from a family of five kids with me being the youngest. We had every opportunity for our older siblings to spoil us.

Our parents collaborated on discipline. I don't remember a warning or any instructions until one day when Fred and I got in trouble. We were rocking on the porch at Fred's house during a rainy spell. The rocker was big enough that Fred and I could sit on the arms, hold the back and the front of the arms while facing each other. We would rock back far enough that it would pause before returning forward. It was quite a ride.

Oscar warned us several times that we were going to turn the rocker over and that when we did, we would break one of the rockers. It happened. We did turn it over. We did break a rocker. We jumped up and sat down on the porch step. We were real quiet, waiting to see what would happen. We knew Fred's dad heard the crash.

He came out and never said a word. He had a razor strap in his hand, the leather strap he used for sharpening his razor. He lifted Fred up by one arm and applied the punishment. I felt sorry for Fred. Then I found out I was next. I ran home crying to tell Mom.

In a short while I returned to Fred's. He was sitting in the shop building pouting. He asked how it went at my house, and laughed when I told him Mom had taken a switch and whipped me again. We hid out until we thought it was safe to go in the kitchen and get a snack.

I'm not sure how old we were when this happened. We had been living on the road for a while, and Fred and I had gotten better acquainted every day of our lives. We knew the rules now. When I talked to Mom she told me that both families had agreed that wherever we were, and whoever we were with, they could discipline us if they thought we needed it. We later found out that Fred's older brothers, B.G. and Garland, could also spank us. I think that was enough people with authority to keep us in line. Goldie's rules had reached an epidemic stage spreading through two families.

When Ida married Fred's brother, Blaine, he became part of the family. Mom got along well with Blaine, and he would listen to her and try to do everything he could to please her.

I remember when we caught the itch. It was a disease that spread more commonly among people who were not clean. It carried a stigma and was an embarrassing thing to have. Jim got it first. I don't believe I ever caught it. Blaine got it really bad. Mom would not let him come in the house during the time he had it.

Blaine used a remedy where he boiled poke root and made a liquid to add to bathwater. He reported that he probably had rather kept on with the battle against the disease than to suffer the extreme burning which followed taking a bath with this remedy. This disease was similar to today's shingles.

Goldie associated everything with cleanliness. Mattie Jo was responsible for my hands being clean before I ate, and I was inspected before I could go to the table. Goldie's rule was that you had to dress yourself as soon as you got out of bed, and have all your clothes on, including shoes and socks before you came to the breakfast table. I remember the trouble I had combing my hair before I made it to the table. I still have that trouble today. My hair will not behave.

This discipline has served me well over the years. The memory of how hard it was to please her, and then the pride I felt when she told me I had done a good job, has encouraged me to do everything she asked over the years.

My sisters, Mattie Jo and Ida, were helpers for Mom. Mattie Jo mothered me if Mom wasn't there. She was my caretaker; Ida was responsible for Nell. Mattie Jo was my favorite when I was learning to dress myself and do other activities that required somebody to help me. She was also there to play with me.

CHAPTER 3

-ᴣ•ᴇ-

D ad had always been very dedicated to the church. He taught Sunday school and led the Wednesday night Bible study. Mom should have realized he was headed toward the ministry. I think he probably discussed it with her before he told the church he was going into the ministry. He became the interim pastor.

Mom was upset. While she enjoyed going to church, she definitely did not want to be a pastor's wife. She said she'd rather mind her own business and let everybody else figure out how they wanted to be Christians. Goldie and I had a lot of discussions over the years about the problems of trying to attend church after Dad became a preacher.

She loved the evangelistic side of it. She could go to a revival, enjoy the singing, and come home and not have any responsibility for the day-by-day ministry. She said that she understood why the Catholic Church decided not to let their priests marry and have families. She told me and Nell that after Dad started preaching, we became orphans because all of his time was taken up by other people and what they needed.

According to Goldie's rules we would probably all get in a groove and never make a change. Except for when she wanted to get away from Bratton, get electricity, and be out where there were people.

Just after Dad went into the ministry, manganese was discovered on the old farm. Dad added the mining business to his ministry. This was a time that Goldie really enjoyed. I've told the story about when Dad invited the investors from Tulsa and Bartlesville, Oklahoma, who were financing the mining operation, to the house for dinner. That was our noon meal.

When I watched the Beverly Hillbillies on TV, I thought of that time when those people came to our house for dinner. Mom cooked a typical country dinner: fried chicken, brown beans, cornbread, and fried potatoes. It was early spring so radishes and onions were just big enough to eat. When these people arrived, dinner was about ready.

I've often wondered what they actually thought when Mom went to the door while they were standing in the yard talking with Dad. She told them rather loudly to wash their hands and get ready to eat. I was eight years old at the time.

I spent six years riding with the geological engineer that did reports for the mining company. Harold Gibbs became a real good friend.

Goldie told me that everybody is just the same. She was not intimidated by those people, and she didn't consider anybody rich or poor. "Good people are just good people, and bad people are just bad people." She would pause and then say, "You just be yourself, Sammy." Now that was a Goldie's rule.

The years after we left Bratton and started mining were probably the most hectic around the house. Dad had tried to start his ministry and it was going well. He held a revival with another minister, Paul Jones. It was outside brush arbor style at the Red Oak Freewill Baptist Church, and ran for most of the summer. I don't actually remember the year, but it was somewhere around 1953.

I don't know how many nights in a row we went to church, but it was amazing how many people attended. They came from all over the country to listen to two different types of Baptist preachers. Dad was a missionary Baptist while Paul Jones was a free will Baptist. The revival was dominated mostly by Pentecostal singing and people that attended various denominations of churches throughout the area.

Goldie would be enthused about going every night, and then she would burn out, ready to stay home for a few days. She wanted to slow down and stay home and rest. Dad was tired. Goldie would share memories of those years. Part of the time she would enthusiastically remember the good times. Other times she would gripe about how much trouble it was, and how some people were so hard to get along with, and all the criticism.

Religion and politics are the main ingredients of

life's struggles. About the time the revival ended, a discussion of predestination began. The idea that everything is preordained by, and is preset by God with people just like puppets. We are going to do whatever we are going to do, and we don't have any control over our preset plan. This was the basis for the argument. The free will people believed that we make a choice to become a Christian and saved from damnation. Other people believed it was preordained, and you were either born a sheep, or you were born a goat. Of course, the goats were all hell bound, and nothing could save them.

Goldie's tolerance for this period of time probably had more influence over my thinking about religion than anything. Our home church, Hickory Hollow Baptist Church, had been started by her uncle, Jess Rose, when he was a circuit riding preacher.

That was the same church we attended when Dad decided he was called into the ministry. This idea of predestination became such a hot argument that the church split. Most of the people left the Baptist church and became a part of the Harriet Assembly of God. Goldie had a lot of family that converted to the Assemblies of God. Her brother, Noble, had married Ed Lack's daughter. Ed was the dominant Assembly of God minister when it started in the area. Aunt Faye Sutterfield and Mom got along well…as long as they didn't try to discuss their religion.

Mom had always had the record books for the Hickory Hollow Baptist Church. Ida was keeping the church clerk records at the time the church split.

They voted Ida out as church clerk. One of the new deacons from the reorganized Independent Baptist Church of Hickory Hollow came to pick up the books that belonged to Hickory Hollow Independent Missionary Baptist church.

Goldie had a key to Ida's house, and we went to her house and picked up the current record books. Mom refused to take the older books that went back to the time when all of her family had started the church.

The same deacon who requested the books came back. He wanted the rest of the books, including the original book. Mom was not about to part with those records. She considered them sacred because a lot of it was in the handwriting of her mother and various other members of the family.

Goldie had spent all that time on Bratton teaching me to control my emotions and to never get upset. This discussion of giving the church books to the reorganized church took place in our front yard. I was about ten years old. Goldie absolutely told the gentleman who came back to get the books what he could do. It didn't end well.

She came back in the house, and Dad tried to tell her that she started a real fight. The argument continued for several months. Thankfully, we didn't have a telephone. Gossip spread much slower, but eventually the sheriff showed up with a warrant to search the house. The new church had sworn out a warrant charging Goldie and Ida with stealing the church records.

The sheriff was a good family friend. Mom acted pretty good, but she made the point clear that he could take the warrant and do whatever he wanted to with it, but she wouldn't let him search through her stuff.

I don't know if I remember other times when Mom was so obstinate about something she believed in. I don't want to portray her as something she wasn't. One of her favorite quotes was, "Everybody's got their faults." I think Goldie demonstrated that her philosophy of always giving everybody consideration for their ideas failed her this time.

Dad was ready to quit from day one. Goldie was not about to give in. This went to the Circuit Court of Searcy County, Arkansas. It is probably the most embarrassing thing our family ever participated in.

Dad hired a lawyer to represent the heritage of Hickory Hollow Missionary Baptist Church, and that the records held by Goldie were placed in her hands by the original founders and could never be transferred to a splinter group that no longer supported the ideas of the founders.

N. J. Hendley was the most prominent lawyer who ever practiced in Marshall, and he and Dad had been friends from the time they were young men. Nobe, as he was known, assured Dad that he could afford to fight this case as long as he wanted to because they'd work out the fees later. I have no idea how this reached a conclusion.

After several days of embarrassing testimony, Mom gave up. Goldie said, "Arvil, tell them they can have the old book, but they can't have any of the little records and notes."

The attorneys went into a conference, and it was

settled. Goldie was going to personally deliver the book that had caused the controversy to the officers of the new Independent Missionary Baptist Church of Hickory Hollow, Arkansas.

This dispute ruined relationships with people in the area. This came after a drought of the 50s caused so many people to leave the area. Several families moved to California or Idaho. Others moved up north to Indiana, Illinois, etc. They moved all over the country, wherever they could find work.

"We lost our neighbors," Dad said, "and then we had a fight with the rest of them. That was Dad's description when he and Mom got ready to rehash the argument.

I don't know if this story has value to Goldie's rules, but it shows a side of her that, if you're going to believe in something, you should stand up for it.

The story of the church dispute took place, I think, shortly after the most exciting time in my life.

Fred Watts and my cousin Harold came over on Sunday after we returned from the cotton patch. They had a report that there was a new girl in our class, and she could read better than I could. I doubted that. I was always cocky confident and full of myself. I believed I could do anything better than anybody else, and that included reading. I told Mom what they said.

Before I left to go to school on Monday, Mom told me, "Sammy, you get along with this new girl."

The first time I saw the new girl she was coming down the sidewalk toward our classroom. She was the prettiest thing I'd ever seen! Her name was

Patricia Treat. She had moved from Oklahoma to Plainview, Arkansas, and then on up to Big Flat and started school in the fourth grade.

When I got home, Mom asked me about the new girl. "Could she really read?"

"Mom, I don't know if she can read a lick, but she's the prettiest thing I've ever seen in my life."

Goldie laughed, and said, "Well, Sammy, you probably won't ever pay attention to how she reads."

The period of time I went from the fourth grade to the seventh grade was when Goldie let me grow up, but at the same time she tried to rein me in if I got out of hand. I had gotten over any intimidation and fears of being around people. Goldie encouraged me to have friendships. She wanted me to take part in school activities. She also wanted me to take up for myself and not ever get run over by anyone. Goldie's big thing was to defend your rights. "If you have to smash somebody's mouth, then smash it, but be big enough to apologize if you made a mistake."

Think about that for a minute. You're supposed to fight if necessary, but then you have to go back and apologize if you think you might be wrong. Goldie's rules to me reflect the struggle that we have as we attempt to live and do things that are right.

I was given privileges. Fred and I were allowed to go camping on Big Creek, at the Odell Morrow farm. We were becoming big boys. We were able to build our own campfire and sleep under a bluff. Odell came by when we first got there on his way to check his cows. He came by later because he thought something might be wrong with one of the cows. He was there the next morning by the time we were up trying to cook breakfast, and he ate with us.

I learned that we really didn't camp by ourselves. Before Dad took us down there he had made a deal with Odell to keep an eye on us. Who knows how many times he checked on us. It could've been several times more than we knew about. It was Mom and Dad's way of taking their hands away and letting us learn to be our own.

Shortly after we went camping, we were coming home from school on the school bus. Fred, his brother, Wesley, and his sister always walked up the hill to catch the school bus at our house. The bus driver saw Mom standing in the yard crying. Wesley got off the bus first, and she told him their dad had died of a heart attack. Wesley broke into a run down the trail toward his house.

Mom, Fred, and his sister walked together through the woods to the Watts house. Nell and I walked along behind them. It's hard to remember a bad time like this, but I remember Fred and me sitting on the rock wall watching the people going in and out of the house. Dad came and took Fred somewhere and talked. I sat on the wall by myself until Mom came over and sat beside me. She didn't say a word. One of her rules was not to talk unless there was something you say that had meaning.

Goldie's rules sustained me in a lot of ways over the years. These few paragraphs are trying to show her in a light that reflects the many sides of her personality.

She was loud. When we went to church at Harriet before the church split up, there were four Sunday school classes in one room. The women's class was in the front, far left. The men's class was in the front, far right. The little kid's class was in the back left, and the young peoples' class was back right. Goldie could disrupt the entire Sunday school if she started laughing or telling a story. She never was a quiet person. As the youngest child of her family, I guess she'd gotten most of the attention because she expected it later in life. I'm the youngest child in our family, so that characteristic may be bred into me.

Goldie had trouble being quiet a lot of the time while the preacher was preaching. I could name the preacher, but I don't think it would be appropriate. One Sunday Mom was sitting next to the preacher's wife, and they were talking loud enough that everybody in the church could hear them. The preacher stopped talking and asked Mom if she could hold it down and at least not talk so loud until he was finished.

I asked Mom, "Do you remember what you said to him?"

"Of course I do," she said. "I told him we listened the first two times you preached the sermon, and now you're preaching it for the fourth time. You need to shut up and let us go home." Everybody laughed at that. And the preacher dismissed church.

CHAPTER 4

-ᘓ•ᘒ-

When I look at the time I spent with my mother, this is the first time I've called her Goldie in this writing. I started to call her Goldie after Pat and I came back to Marshall and I worked as a Farm Bureau insurance agent. When I tried to explain who I was to people, if I mentioned Goldie, they knew her. She had worked in restaurants and at different jobs in Marshall and had become acquainted with a lot of people.

Everybody remembers as they were growing up how things change just before you get to puberty. I spent several of those years with my mother. Goldie was my best friend, my partner, and took care of me constantly. I've been with her as we gathered the vegetables to cook for dinner when it was just the two of us on Bratton, and I stood by the stove as her helper while she cooked. Without really realizing it, I learned a lot about how to prepare everything that we ate. She was fearful of me becoming too much of a mother's boy, and insisted that I get out with Dad and my brother and do things that men did.

The truth is she was more able to do some things in the fields, and working, than anybody I ever knew. We gathered corn, we dug potatoes, we cut wood, we did all the chores regardless of who normally would do that sort of thing. There were no male female duties around an old homestead. You just did the work that needed to be done.

As I entered the middle school years and began to play basketball, baseball in the summertime, and participating in every activity the school had to offer, Mom accompanied me in all these activities.

She was big on staying busy. She believed that idle hands and idle minds would find mischief. I read constantly, and I still do, but Mom made sure that I read everything I could get my hands on. I read the story of Davy Crockett when I was about eight or nine years old. I didn't realize he was going to die at the Alamo until I got to the end of the book. Mattie Jo laughed when I finished the book, laid it on the floor and began crying. I said I would've never read that thing if I'd known how it was going to end.

That is a good example of all the things you learn in life. There are more bad endings that we remember longer than the good endings we reminisce about. The times that school had problems, and the times that the churches had problems probably taught us more lessons that stuck with us better than the good times.

The six years from the fourth grade 'til the tenth

grade in school was a time that Goldie spent more time trying to correct things she did than teaching me things. She wanted me to get out and go places and do things, but if she heard that I had done something I shouldn't have...and I did...well, let's just say I learned a lot!

I got in with a group of boys during a church service where Dad was preaching, and we didn't come in the church house and sit down. We made a trip to one of the local boy's farm and had a watermelon party. The way I told the story, the way I remembered, was not true. We got caught, and turns out the guy that led us to the watermelons had totally misrepresented the owner.

I thought Mom was going to hang me for several days after we got caught. I had to apologize to Dad's congregation for having participated in that watermelon raid. The longest walk I ever took was from the seat I was sitting in, to the front of the church, stepping up on the stage and turning to apologize.

I don't remember a word that I said. I probably said it through tears, red-faced, and everything that goes with embarrassment. On the way home nobody said a word for a while, then Mom told me she was proud of me. She said I had taken responsibility for what I had done. That's a hard lesson in life to do like Goldie said and admit you're wrong and step up and share your failures.

There's not much of real substance about growing up as a teenager. Pride in our clothes, trying to look our best, making sure we were part of the right crowd, and then keeping a lid on our confidence to the point that we are likeable. On one hand they want you to step up and be outgoing, and on the other hand they want you to be humble enough that you never become a smart aleck. Goldie was good at bragging on me at the right time and building my ego, and then jerking the props out from under me and bringing me back down to earth, and telling me that I needed to be just an ordinary, calm person, that I never needed to brag.

Nobody wants to listen to a person that is full of themselves, or somebody that constantly corrects other folks. Goldie told me early on that would be my biggest struggle. I guess when people talked to her about me they would always tell her something that she felt like I needed to work on, and that I would be better off if I could correct it.

When I hear people talk about the good old days, how bad it was, or how good it was, I always think about how everything we do is a percentage. There are always enough good things for us to enjoy in any given day that when the day ends, we've had a good day. And there's always opportunities that we failed to take advantage of, and things that didn't turn out right, so that if we exaggerate those, it becomes a bad day.

Along about the eighth grade, Goldie spent most of her time trying to balance the good with the bad. When she would talk about times that had gone by and were now in memories of yesterday, she would point out the things she liked. She would talk about how great it was to sit on the porch and visit with people on Bratton because we didn't get to see them every day, and when they did come to see us, there was a lot to learn and a lot to catch up on, and that was a really good time.

She would talk about how hard it'd been, how cold it was when we had to get out and do our chores, and how hard it was to carry water from the spring to the house. When I listen today to people, I am reminded of Goldie saying that the best of times always include the worst of times.

During this period of time my older sisters and brother had children. They were my first nephews and nieces, and Goldie's first grandchildren. As a grandfather today, I know how she felt the first time she held Mark Alan Watts, her first grandchild. I can understand the smile she got on her face when she saw Debbie Pemberton for the first time. I also know how she felt when Rita Fay Wilson showed up at our house for the first time. These were the good times. During that same time, in 1959 my granny Stacy Sutterfield died and was buried.

This is what Goldie's rules and teachings have caused me to learn about life. She would say, "Don't celebrate too long because when the bad things come, the memories of the good times will carry you through the bad times."

Pat and I graduated from high school in 1962 as members of a class of 12 at Big Flat. Pat and her family went to Idaho for the summer, and I went to Russellville, Arkansas, to work before I started college in the fall. I was not prepared for this change in living. You think you know a lot growing up. But Goldie wasn't there to cook my meals, have my clothes done for me, and to just guide me in the direction I should go. I was homesick.

Sam and Pat going on a date.
Taken in 1962 at Big Flat, in Pat's front yard.

I thought about how I'd wake up and could smell the biscuits. I could hear Dad trying to sing as he helped Mom cook breakfast. He never could sing any better than I could, and that's awful. But I got out of bed, put my clothes on, and got ready to go and sit down for that breakfast meal. And when I got there I caught up on the things that happened the

SAM PEMBERTON

day and night before. Then it was off to school for me and off to work for Dad, and I had somebody pointing me in the direction I needed to go. Goldie never had any trouble coming up with what I was going to do.

Now I was an adult, and working to make my own money. I was trying to manage my own clothes, and I found out I wasn't nearly as prepared for this adult life that I had been looking forward to as I thought. It was always good to go home to Mom.

It was a very short time from when Pat and I graduated from high school until we were making plans to get married. I discussed all of this with my mom, and trust me, I think she's always liked Pat better than she did me. I don't know of any wife that ever had a better relationship with her mother-in-law than Patricia had with Goldie.

As I related earlier, I learned to cook standing at Mom's elbow while she stirred the pot. Our families knew each other well and Mom was aware that Pat had never done much cooking. My brother, Jim, and most of the men in the family had criticized their wives when they got married about how they couldn't do anything. Mom called me in a couple of weeks before Pat and I got married, and she said, "Sammy, I've got to talk to you."

I had no idea what she was about to say. She started out with, "You've got to make me a promise." I still had no idea what she was gonna say. Then she said, "When you and Pat gets married, I don't care what she cooks or how she cooks it, you stay out of the kitchen and you eat it when she's got it cooked, and don't you ever say a word." She got in front of me, and she said, "Now, did you hear what I said?"

"Yeah, Mom, I heard you."

"Will you remember that as long as you live? That's how it is."

Over the years I have told Pat that story several times. We had been married 25 to 30 years before I ever went into the kitchen to cook. I told her I could make Mom's chocolate rolls.

Goldie's rules are strong. They give you a guilty conscience if you break one, and if you make a promise, you're scared to death of what'll happen if you break it.

Her instructions have served my and Pat's marriage well.

Over the years all of my brothers and sisters at one time or another had some sort of problem with Goldie. I'm not saying she and I never had a problem. There were times when reaching a consensus on a situation involved considerable discussion. Goldie and I had a special relationship because with me being the youngest, I was the one she passed on the benefits to of her experience with my older brothers and sisters.

She was talking one time about Jim asking her a question, just any generic question. She had learned that if he asked a question and she answered "you may be right" that she could expect to hear from one of the other children that she had said exactly the contents of Jim's question. She and I discussed this quite a bit. Think about that. When someone asks you a question and you say "you may be right" it gives consent in their mind to repeat the question as a stated fact that you agree with.

I think today we can relate this to the "like" button on Facebook. The other day Pat and I had a conversation about something I read to her from Facebook, and I told her I had "liked" it. She said, "That's the same thing you told me years ago about when Jim would ask you something, and later quoted you as having said it." I have to agree with her.

According to Goldie's rules we would never be able to maintain relationships with anyone if we are totally honest. "Sammy, if you don't tell enough lies to protect your business, you will be friendless and divorced." She laughed when she said that. She went on to say that answering "that's not your business" was not a very good way of carrying on a conversation. Tact usually requires that we allow people to keep the impression they have in any given situation. Assumptions are made about everything based on conversation, clothing, vehicles, and anything else people have around them, including friends and houses.

Mom would look at people and make comments privately to me that made me wonder what she told my brothers and sisters when I wasn't around. She always told me, "If you gossip, expect people to gossip about you." She would go on to say, "We all love gossip. I don't think there's anything wrong with listening to it just as long as you don't spread it where it doesn't need to be spread."

I never have deciphered that one. I assume, and I use that word cautiously, that she meant to be careful who you repeat it to, and to make sure you don't add anything to it that can be traced back to you.

When she lived at Harriet, she got her first ever telephone after I was in college. When I came home, she would start to tell me something, and the opening line would be, "Sammy, you won't believe what I heard on that telephone." She wasn't talking about *her* phone calls. She was talking about the ones she listened in to on their eight-party telephone line.

I asked her if she thought it was okay to listen in.

"Why not? They shouldn't be saying anything if they don't want me to hear it. They all know that we are on the same line."

Everybody on that party line was family. I hadn't been there long until the phone rang and she answered. I listened as she talked. I don't remember who the call was from, but then she asked, "J. W., have you picked up the phone?" She told whoever it was she was talking to, "If he gets on here, we will ask him."

I also remember that as the call progressed, the number of people online continued to increase. Finally, she said, "Somebody's got to hang up. There are so many on here we can't hear each other."

That was a version of today's Facebook where everybody could hear and find out what was going on. That was a special time. It only lasted three to four years before Dad passed away, and Mom moved away from Harriet.

CHAPTER 5

-⅜•⅗-

These writings so far have covered a period of time from October 27, 1913, to about September 1962. This forty-nine-year period of Goldie's life can be broken up into the time that she lived on Big Creek, and then the time she lived on Bratton Creek after she was married and had her children.

I didn't spend as much time as I should have described her life as a child. Those were the days of changing from horse and buggies to the automobile. I have no idea when Grandpa Sutterfield bought his first car. I do remember Dad laughing about the time they had borrowed Grandpa's car. Uncle Donald Davis, J. W.'s dad, was the driver, and the steering wheel came off and they had a wreck. A wreck in those days was minor because there were no roads, and it was impossible to go fast enough to cause a lot of damage.

When they got automobiles, they were still traveling the trails that constantly crossed back and forth along the streams that made automobile travel next to impossible. Crossing the stream of water through the gravel was no problem with a horse drawn vehicle. But when the cars tried to travel the same trail they were constantly getting stuck in the gravel as they tried to cross the streams.

I was told a story about an automobile getting stuck in a stream. A wagon could be pushed by lifting it through the gravel. One of the automobile passengers tried to give it a push by getting ahold of one of the spoked wheels on the rear. When the driver pushed down on the accelerator, the wheel spun and threw the fellow a considerable distance out in front of the car. Supposedly the fellow's comment was, "I learned something you don't do with an automobile."

This is one of the few stories I can remember Mom or Dad either one telling about the years they were dating. They married when Mom was not quite sixteen years old. Dad was born in the Landis community, some five to six miles south and east from Mom's home. He had moved with his family and was living on a farm owned by Grandpa Sutterfield.

Grandpa Sutterfield was a whiskey producer. During the Prohibition days he operated some illegal stills along the banks of Big Creek, and my dad was making whiskey for him when he met my mom. Goldie always said, "Dad never thought it was any of the government's business."

I cannot relate to this period of time nor make a moral judgment of right or wrong about what my dad and grandfather did at the time. Goldie told me things. It never seemed that she was proud of it, or embarrassed by it. In later years she related stories about how Granny Stacy did not like having people around when Grandfather Sutterfield was in the moonshine business.

The school system consisted of grades one through eight, and operated three months in the summer. She went to school in a one room schoolhouse, "Cedar Grove," across the creek from where Mom grew up. This was typical at that time.

I wanted to share enough of her time that she was growing up to give some idea of what influenced her to believe what she believed, and why she chose to pass those beliefs on to me.

Before I started college I went to work at the job I still do, in the construction business. After Pat and I got married, we wanted to have children immediately. We had our first child before we had been married a full year. Goldie supported us in doing this. Her values were always dominated by her love for family. Being lonesome on Bratton wasn't about being remote as much as it was about not being around people. I remember after we moved, we were close enough for her to literally have a conversation with J. W. by yelling back and forth across the hollow.

We never had a telephone at Harriet while I was growing up. J. W. would walk out in his yard and yell, "Aunt Goldie!" They would yell back and forth while walking toward each other. They were able to conduct a loud conversation at quite a distance. I don't know if this is common among people living close together that didn't have the benefit of a telephone. When I tell people that they yelled across the hollow, I believe they find that unbelievable.

With all of this, I'm trying to relate and create an image of my mother. Most people exaggerate anything they tell. I'm guilty of that. I know my prejudices cause me to portray her in a light that no one else could see.

When Pat and I were married, there were very few people's advice more trusted than my mother's and Pat's dad, Vernon Treat.

Pat and I were in St. Louis when I got a call from Mom that Dad was sick. Pat and I had been home for Christmas before that call and he hadn't felt well, but we couldn't get him to go to the hospital. He'd suffered a tick bite in November during deer season and had developed a severe inflammation in his left leg. Mom had taken him to the hospital in Leslie, Arkansas.

Goldie's life changed rather quickly in a couple of weeks after that. My dad passed away and left Goldie living alone in the house on the road, the house that J. W. had built. Goldie never learned to drive, and here she is living out in the country. The only farm they have left is 80 acres about a mile from the house. And Mom had a few animals that she was responsible for. She was living alone in a house that only had wood heat and no plumbing.

We had always lived in these primitive conditions and thought nothing of it. The old kerosene lamp had been replaced by electric lights when we moved up the road to get electricity, and other than adding a TV, that's about all the conveniences that had ever been added to Mom's lifestyle.

I had taken a job in Florida and was leaving shortly to go down there. Mom decided to rent a house in Marshall, move out there and cook in the cafes. Her plan worked. When I returned from Florida, she had sold the house and the farm at Harriet, and she was working. I could tell Mom was adjusting as well as possible.

According to Goldie's rules we accept what is and we look forward to the best possibilities of what could be. She seemed happier than I expected her to be. It hadn't been long enough for me to talk about losing my dad and move on, but when I visited with her, she was ready to get on with her life. Pat and I tried to include her in all the things that we did, and I would pick her up and take her with us to any special singing or anything that was going on at the church. That's when I called her on Saturday and got a shock!

Goldie's purpose in life was to fill her time and never have a void where she wasn't doing something. Years before she and Dad had a couple of near and dear friends that they visited with, and went to church with, and were really close to. I called Mom and told her I would pick her up and take her to a singing on a Saturday night at our church, and she said, "I can't go. I'm having company."

I said, "Well, if you're having company, we'll

just come and visit with you."

After several exchanges back and forth, I found out that Radus Drewry was Mom's company. His wife had passed away a few months before Dad, and he and Mom had started visiting after she moved to Marshall. He worked in a store. Mom went by there after her job, and they struck up a friendship. Of course, this was a man that Mom had known for years.

Goldie's new life was quite an adjustment, and it extended her rules in a lot of directions. Here were these two huge families with grandchildren, and some of the grandchildren were teenagers and had friends in the whole family on both sides. That could not be integrated into one unit. According to Mom's rules we could come at Thanksgiving. We could come and visit if we called and gave notice. I didn't have a problem with it, but some of the family had real difficulties accepting the change. It's sad to have to go through a change that eliminates your relationships as you knew them. I don't want to turn this into a pity party because Goldie made the adjustments she had to. My daughter, Sherri, never knew a grandfather other than Papa Radus. She was born in 1970, and at this time I was living in a house that Pat and I had built at Harriet out in the woods. Pat felt about that place about like Goldie did Bratton.

Mom's rules that she had to make to deal with her new circumstances, and to deal with all of the family were hard for her to enforce. There were not as many difficulties as you would expect, and she dealt with things quite well, and got along with her new partner really well.

Mom would take Sherri and go to the farm that Radus had, and fish in the creek while he worked tending to his cows. Sherri loved it, and she and Mom developed a relationship that stuck in Sherri's mind 'til this day. I've never discussed with Sherri about whether Mom tried to set rules for Sherri's life or not. I would bet she did.

Things became normal and mundane with me switching careers and becoming an insurance agent there in Marshall. I could have lunch with Mom, and I could have relationships with people that I had been around for a good many years. Goldie's advice and instructions aided me greatly when I changed my career. If I had a problem with someone, Mom could give me the history of why. She would remember a problem that had to do with someone over a church fuss, or when he worked in the tax assessor's office, or any of this type of thing. A couple of times when I went out to service an insurance policy and they realized who I was, they came into the office and cancelled their insurance without a word of explanation.

I wrote earlier about how grudges had been carried all the way from Tennessee to Arkansas, and I had been raised to leave them alone because they were not good folk. I was amazed to learn that it still applied to me as I tried to sell insurance. If I called on one of these people that my dad or grandfather or anyone else that had had a dispute with, they didn't want to do business with me, either.

We can laugh about it, or we can deny it, but

Goldie always said, "The heaviest load you will ever carry is a grudge." It's hard to explain built-in prejudices that we acquire as a child and keep hidden, but they come out in circumstances that renew the grudge.

Goldie and I spent a lot of time as we visited together through the years while Pat and I lived there in Searcy County. We discussed how bad everything is hindered by our inability to move on and live according to Christian rules instead of stirring in the problems of the past.

I admire the way Mom adjusted after Dad died, and started a new life, but nothing is ever totally forgotten. Forgiveness lasts as long as we keep it fresh in our hearts and in our minds. Goldie told me, "Forgiveness has to be maintained." That's the hardest rule to live by for all of us. We all have a Goldie's rule that hits the things we have developed in our consciousness that guides us in our daily lives.

The time from when I graduated from high school, trying to make a living and develop a life that Pat and I could enjoy, was a tough period. We had grown up with the Big Flat High School, gone to college for a while, got married, returned back to where we grew up, and started sending our children to school in the Marshall school system.

One day I realized our children were going to have the same choice we had when graduating from high school. They could go off to college, and then they would have to find another place to live, and to get a job. Goldie's rules always look back to the time where she was born. She had a desire for things to have never changed, that she could have lived in the area where she grew up, and stayed close to her family. She had done it as well as anybody could, but there was still a huge amount of people—friends and relatives—that had left and scattered all over the country.

I know how scary it was to adjust to living in cities. I understand why Goldie never would agree to move away from Marshall. She lived near or in Marshall her entire life until her kidneys failed, and she had to move to be close to her dialysis treatment.

As I enter the longest and most detailed part of her life and her story, we have to look at the attitude of becoming a senior citizen.

I am living the final stages of the instructions Goldie lived by her last days. They have become the conclusion of living by Goldie's rules.

CHAPTER 6

-ઝ•ફ-

Goldie's life settled into a routine after she and Radus Drewsy married. While it was awkward to adjust to a new family situation, we all got to the point where we understood our role. While things could never return to normal after we lost Dad, Mom was making the best of her new life.

The younger grandkids, like Sherri, were able to accept a new Papa easily. The older grandkids never did.

Mom continued to work in the restaurant and did so well that she became renowned for her doughnuts. There was a time when she almost stayed busy making those doughnuts at home and people picked them up to sell in their restaurants.

When she reached an age that she was old enough to work on an old folks program, called Green Thumb, I think, she started working at the high school in the most natural place for her to work—the kitchen.

One day I got a call from the school superintendent, but before I could answer he told my secretary that he might need me to come to the high school. Within a few minutes they called back and told me to cancel that.

I called the school and talked to the school secretary to ask if there was a problem with Sherri. She had had a problem earlier in the year with a young lady trying to correct her. And Sherri, somewhat like her granny, would defend her territory and not allow anybody to get in her face. She had a fight. I had never been called to the school before, and I was not real happy about having to go that time. I never anticipated when I got a call this time that it would be because my mother had an altercation with the head cook!

When the day was over I was rather anxious to go by Mom's and hear the story about what happened at school. I had no trouble getting her to tell me the story. "Sammy, I've never let anybody tell me how to cook something that I've been cooking all my life." She went on to say that she had decided to make the school kids some of her doughnuts.

The head cook came over and asked Mom what she thought she was doing. I have no idea why my mother thought she could take over authority and cook a batch of her doughnuts. I have no idea how the conversation proceeded, but from the reports I got, the two women were fussing in the kitchen loud enough that the entire school could hear them. And that was why I got the call from the superintendent.

As I write this, I'm amused that I had a call for a fight that my daughter was in at school, and then I have a call for a fight my mother had. Goldie always made life interesting.

Mom worked as long as she was able. After she started working on the senior program, she was off every Saturday. Jim would come to the office for an hour or so, and when my appointments for the day were finished, we would go to Mom's to visit. We had a lot of good times stopping by to see her, both by appointment and unannounced.

One day as we started up the walk to the front door, Mom came to the door and said, "You boys get right back in that truck and leave. I don't have time to mess with you today. I'm getting ready to go somewhere." That was Goldie. According to her rules, it was only being honest to tell people when you didn't want to do something. Jim and I were almost 50 years old and Mom was in her 70s, and we were not surprised that she would run us off because Radus was there and there was something she'd rather do.

When we visited with her, she would tell us stories of the week comparable to the one about her and the cook getting into it at work. Mom could get so emotional and irate telling the story. One day she was very loud and adamant telling us something when the phone rang. She stopped and answered the phone in her sweetest possible voice and talked to one of her nieces. When the finished the phone all she said, "Where was I?" She resumed her story in the same rage and at the same point she had been before the phone rang.

Goldie seated. Behind her: Sam, Nell, Mattie, Ida.

Over the years Jim and I discussed how much emotional control she had to be able to do that. Goldie's rule was that you could compartmentalize your attitude and treat good people in a good way, and treat other people however you thought they deserved.

I don't think I've ever been able to completely isolate an opinion and not allow it to affect my other ideas. I am pretty good at not sharing every emotion that I feel with people that I don't have any reason to share it with. She maintained her happiness by not allowing things that bothered her to corrupt everything else that she did. Troubles come to all of us. There are times we get upset about something, and it's hard not to share that and talk about it to others.

Mom and I had a lot of conversations after she got into her 70s about the trials and tribulations she'd experienced, and in the things that were left in front of her. She had to start dealing with Alzheimer's when Radus started having mental lapses. She visited with me about it several times confidentially before there was ever any medical diagnosis.

In Goldie's opinion, "Life can prepare us for a lot of things, but nothing can prepare you for living with someone you love that comes down with Alzheimer's." The next few years became a struggle. It got to the point that it was more than Mom could handle. She said she definitely had to have a break. We decided to buy a mobile home and park it in Marshall next door to a friend that Mom had worked with for years in restaurants. This gave her a place to go. We discussed this with Radus, and a daughter who lived out west came to stay with him while Mom took a break.

According to Goldie's rules, she believed in facing something head-on. While she was taking a break from living with Radus she never intended that their lives together were over. I had several discussions with different members of Radus' family, and we agreed that Mom didn't need to be responsible for his care. I contacted an attorney to ask him the best way to handle it and he said we should appoint his children as guardians. We did.

At the end of that thirty-day period the two children who had been appointed guardians sued Mom for divorce, alleging that she had deserted their dad.

We had never been blindsided by anything worse. Going into details would not be useful, but this certainly showed the true character of my mother.

"Sammy, I don't know of anything that's ever hurt me any worse, but my life has gotta go on and I'm just going to make the best of this."

To this day I am amazed at her ability to accept things that she knew she couldn't change. If I could incorporate one thing of her rules into my life permanently and abide by it, it would be the ability to assess, accept what cannot be changed, and move on with my life.

After this, Mom settled in to living in the house trailer. But she had one problem. She wanted to be able to get outside and do things. She was not able to mow her yard and it wasn't part of her deal, but she called me one night and said, "Sammy, you gotta do something."

When I asked why she told me that I needed to build a deck or something so she could get outside and sit and not be cooped up in that trailer all the time.

Goldie and Sam's wife Pat in the mobile home

Goldie, taken the same day.

Goldie and food

Goldie in her trailer.

I was home from work for a few days. I had left the insurance business and was back into construction work full time. I had already planned to take a couple of weeks off between jobs.

At Mom's trailer we started out with a deck that would allow her to sit outside. When we finished we had a sunroom with windows and screens and a roof. It was completely winterized so she could sit out there any time she wanted to.

The porch, or sunroom, became the new visiting place for Goldie and me. She reminisced as far back as her memory would take her, and I listened to all the things she chose to talk about. We dug up bones from the bad things. We laughed and discussed the good things. And we tried to come up with a plan to go forward.

I had to tell Goldie that when Sherri graduated from high school Pat and I were going to relocate, probably to Nixa or Springfield, Missouri. While I had been gone for periods of time before, working all over the country, I had never completely moved away. Pat and I had spent a year in the St. Louis area—the year Dad died. We had lived in North Little Rock a couple of years. But basically, Mom knew that I had always planned to come back home to Marshall. We had been there over twelve years. We had lost Pat's dad and my dad; we were the caretakers of Pat's mom and Goldie. When she heard about this move, Goldie cried.

According to Goldie's rules I was breaking every one of them by not putting her and Pat's mom first. She said we needed to just stay and take care of our parents. I don't think it was any good or bad choice, it was just something we had to do.

Before we left, Mom and I discussed everything she needed to do to survive as an old person. We went through the steps of what to do when she had to have help in the house. After we left Mom rode the bus to the senior center to visit and eat lunch. She had an in-home health care worker. She took advantage of every opportunity that was provided to her to maintain her life. Another one of Goldie's rules: "You do whatever you have to do to survive."

Taken after Goldie moved into her mobile home.
Ida Horton, Nell Lawrence, Goldie, Mattie, Sam.

The strongest will we have is to survive. Mom believed that recognizing the circumstances and making the needed adjustment with the fewest complaints possible was the best way to survive.

She became friends with Wesley Smith who was the state representative. Mom had known his family

all of their lives. He kept her i
program that she was eligible for.
was the County Clerk through
political career Mom relied on hin
what she needed to do. A lot of tin
me Wesley told her to go see B
Services.

Regardless of what you think about our system, Goldie believed it was necessary to provide for her. While her children could do some things it was not possible for us to provide her with health care and all the services she received while she lived in the trailer.

The visits that Goldie and I had in the later years she still lived in Marshall we not as frequent as she would've liked. I justified it by saying it was all I had tine for. We had a good time on those visits. We scheduled a family reunion a couple of times a year, and when we didn't have a family reunion we visited by opportunity.

I remember on one visit we started our conversation and I couldn't think of somebody's name. She couldn't either. "Sammy, we are going to stop this right now. We're not spending our entire visit trying to think of somebody's name. If I can't think of it and I'm telling the story, and you can't thing of a name and you're telling the story, we're just going to skip it and go on."

That is a Goldie's rule. Pat and I try to apply it today. When we can't think of somebody's name, we both laugh and say, "Well, it's time to move on." Goldie was right. We don't need to spend our time trying to think of names.

CHAPTER 7

-3•6-

G oldie again made adjustments to move on and do the best she could. She survived rather well for a period of time, until she reached the point she needed someone close. We met and had several discussions about what the next move should be.

In 1995 my brother, Jim, died from bone cancer. Mom and I made several trips to visit him while he was in the hospital at Mountain Home, Arkansas. He spent most of his time in the nursing home adjoining the hospital. At this point Goldie was 82 years old.

As for surviving financially, Goldie's rule was, "Always live within your means." My mother and my Uncle Ollie had the most influence over how I view finances. Uncle Ollie said, "If you think you need something, wait a week. If you can do without it for a week, don't buy it, you never needed it in the first place." Mom was almost as bad. Her rule was, "Don't ever buy anything unless you thought about it, shopped for it everywhere to get the best price, and got something that would last for a long time."

She was not a hoarder, but I have things that was hers that are almost as old as I am. If Pat and I had not lost our house to fire when we lived in Harriet, I would have books and keepsakes that would go back to the 1840s.

I use the old saying, "Waste not want not." People old enough to have gone through the Great Depression and World War II along with the drought in the 1950s understood getting through the hard times. When Mom was able to get on Social Security, work on the Greens program after she retired, receive healthcare through Medicare, she though it was the greatest deal you could ever have. She remembered the times when people had to leave because they got to the point they absolutely could not provide for themselves.

Goldie had never experienced poverty. When you apply the rules that she and Uncle Ollie always lived by, you don't spend your money unnecessarily; and consider that they always had a way to make some money to get by. People that lived in the hills of east Searcy County were much poorer than the people that lived around Marshall and along Bear Creek and the Buffalo River. While there was a lot more timber work, the farmland was actually a lost cause. Strawberries and tomatoes were crops that could be grown successfully, but no big commercial operation was possible on those gravel hillsides. Still, the people that understood the potential and how much they could plan on, and lived within their means, survived and did well.

Goldie's rule, "If you live a life where you are constantly comparing your situation to somebody else, you will never be satisfied." That's the reason she could accept things, like when the situation became unsolvable with the family of her second husband, and she had to move on. She did. Mentally, if she stopped to think, she would make trips back to her childhood remembering the good times. She journeyed on up through the 20s when she met my dad. Then she went through the years that she raised her family.

As the youngest child I can't write with authority about the time before we lived on Bratton. But I can recall the up-and-down period of time emotionally and economically that included the time when Dad mined for manganese.

When you look back at your life like Goldie and I did whenever I visited her in the trailer and she wanted to reminisce, it was always a combination of good and bad. "Life goes on." That is Goldie's rule.

When she began to lose her health to the point that her mobility was failing her, and her ability to take care of herself, and getting up and down the steps to the trailer were becoming too much, she was smart enough to realize that. And now that I'm in the same age bracket that she was at that time, I realize how worrisome it is to realize you're not ever going to be able to go back and recover all of your physical abilities again. "Making the best of it" is the rule we have to apply without any other choice. Mom was good at recognizing and assessing the situation as it actually was. The five Ps of success are "Prior planning prevents poor performance."

Recognizing the difference between a dream and a plan was something she was good at.

"Without a vision the people perish" is a saying based on Scripture principles. I listened as Mom and Dad discussed what it meant to have a vision. A vision includes as many known factors as is possible to see for a decision you are making. A dream sees the end of the rainbow. A vision sees all the problems plus the opportunities available to make a dream come true. Big corporations spend a lot of money on research to develop a product and to be able to see the market for it, and the cost to take it to market before they start production.

Goldie taught me that our lives need to be run like a corporation. We need to be able to see all the assets, including people, that are valuable to us as friends and as helpers as we go along in life. When she and I talked about Pat and me getting married, she pointed out that she thought Pat would be a good wife, a good worker, and that we would have a good laugh. Whenever she got to the point that she had to make a decision, she evaluated what was best for her to do.

In the later years she was pragmatic about what would work for her, and she made the decision to move out of the trailer and into the apartments at Heritage Place. She had lost two children, my brother Jim and my sister Ida. She was still mourning the loss of these children.

Goldie and grandchildren.
Front row: Teresa Weeks, Debbie Baron, Goldie and
Sherri Conrad.
Back row: Steve Lawrence, Tracy Ward, Mark Watts.

Goldie with her granddaughters.
Front row: Goldie, Rita Miles.
Back row: Cheryl Freeman, Sandy Wright, Debbie Baron,
Tracie Ward, Sherri Conrad.

Now she would have people around her, which as always important to Goldie, and she would be able to get to the senior center easier, and all the conveniences would be much better than having to walk to the post office and climb in and out of that trailer.

Goldie was always about being happy. She wanted to tell a good story and have a good time every day.

After much discussion she sold the trailer and made the move. She adjusted in a hurry. In a few short months she had developed a friendship with Virginia Harness. While they had known each other most of their lives, they hadn't done anything together. Now they had become friends.

I'll never forget when Goldie told me they had gone to Mountain View, Arkansas, in Virginia's old jalopy to the senior center. And danced. While Mom still lived in the trailer she had met a friend, a male friend who liked to dance. When she and Virginia went to Mountain View Mom danced with him most of the time.

That story shows that Mom actually lived by her rules, making the best of the situation. Things are seldom what we would prefer they be. There's never enough time or money to do everything we want to do. But according to Goldie's rules, just take advantage of every opportunity and enjoy life.

However, not long after losing those two children her health began to fail.

Dr. Jennings, her primary care doctor, had made an appointment in Conway, Arkansas, with a kidney specialist. We made the trip to Conway. I did not go in with her to the appointment. After the examination they ran some more tests.

I could tell from her expression it was not good news.

I did not say anything as we got into the car and started driving back home. I knew she would tell me in her own time.

"Sammy, you can't live without your kidneys, can you?"

"No, Mom, you can't."

We sat quiet as we drove to a fast-food place, I don't remember where. It was somewhere in Greenbrier just north of Conway on the way back to Marshall. We didn't have much of a discussion. As loud and talkative as Goldie's personality always was, when she became worried she became silent. We finished eating and got back in the car.

She relayed more of what the doctor had said. She had asked why she couldn't get a kidney transplant. She got real silent for quite a while, and then said, "He told me they cut off at age 85." She paused and said, "I don't think that's fair."

I had always admired her will to live. This time I could see that she was viewing this as a death sentence. I was dumbfounded. I didn't really know how to talk to my 85-year-old mother. She had just been given the news that she was headed for dialysis. She knew that it wouldn't last over 30 months. Mom had always said that attitude controls our destiny, that philosophy has been expressed as the power of positive thinking, that whatsoever a man thinketh so is he. I've heard it said a lot of different ways, but having a positive outlook has to be beneficial because after every situation she went through she always looked at it in the most positive way possible.

We had a discussion about if she were able to get a transplant, would she be able to do it? Who would be her donor?

"You would be my donor?"

I never answered her. I have to admit the thought of going to surgery to donate a kidney is something I had never even considered. To this day I regret not telling her I would have been willing to do it.

Goldie stayed at The Heritage until she had to go on dialysis. She tried to do it by going to Mountain Home three days a week. She had to be there at 4 o'clock in the afternoon. That was the only time they could get her on the machine. Social Services furnished her transportation. This is the one thing, of the few things I know Mom had to face, that was too much for her.

I would call her before the driver came to pick her up, and then I would call her several times until I was sure she'd made it back home. This was wintertime and the driver had to deal with those crooked roads from Marshall to Mountain Home. Mom rode in the backseat because the driver had his wife with him.

To make a long story short, Mom couldn't do it.

She was put in the hospital at Mountain Home, and had to have a port put in her shoulder to attach to the dialysis. The surgery did not go well. She suffered excessive bleeding and had to be hospitalized.

Pat and I went down in the middle of the night

and met my niece Debbie, and Robert Baron, at the hospital. My sister, Maddie Jo and her husband, Estes, joined us later.

Mom always told me that she thought life would end easily if you were prepared to handle it.

There is no practice for it. It just happened. I think we entered a state of shock at her passing. I wasn't ready to look at it just yet, especially since it was the gal that set the tone for my entire life. Goldie had not written a rule for this. Neither has anybody else.

I was amazed at the end at how well she handled having to go into the nursing home. She was admitted to the nursing home adjoining Baxter Reginal Medical Center. I don't think I had ever really seen her depressed. I've seen her aggravated a lot of times. I've seen her when she was demanding what she wanted and insisting things get done immediately. But she was truly depressed while she was in Baxter rehab at Mountain Home, Arkansas.

I visited her every Sunday afternoon. She wanted me to do her laundry, to take it to the laundromat, the cleanest one in Mountain Home and do it myself. "I don't want these people mixing my laundry with everybody else's," she said. That was one of Goldie's rules: Don't share other people's nastiness.

Some of this was enjoyable. I got to share some really good times with her. I learned firsthand what it was like to experience the inevitable things in life.

She decided that she wanted to move to Rogers, Arkansas, so she could be close to Maddie Jo and her granddaughters. We made arrangements to move her to a nursing home there. It was the best thing we could do at the time.

When we got Mom settled in, we didn't know that one of her primary caregivers was going to be her grandniece, Annette MacDonell, who was a granddaughter of Theodore and Zelma Sutterfield. Theodore was Mom's cousin, and Zelma was Dad's sister. We also did not realize that Norma Carlton, another granddaughter and Annette's sister, was a beautician and lived in the area. While my sisters and my nieces did a good job, these cousins stepped up and made Mom's days as pleasant as possible.

Mom adjusted quickly. "if I had known how easy it was to live in a nursing home," she said, "I would have checked myself in a long time ago."

The last photo taken of Goldie; at the nursing home in Rogers.

CHAPTER 8

-9•6-

After Mom passed away January 2001, I began to think about the life that she had lived. The idea for this book about her and her rules is the result of a conversation I had with her just before she died.

When I spent the day with her in October 2000, she realized that her time was short. While we visited I listened to her trying to make sense of all the things that happened to her over the years. I realized that it was a system she had lived by, but it was more than that. It was realizing that our place in life is not set by destiny as much as by our determination to live according to a set of values.

Survival is the strongest instinct we possess. According to Goldie's rules, the thing that makes us able to survive is work. Simply hard work. Also, our ability to interact with others. We gain the most in life by making sure we make good choices. I strongly believe in Providence, but being prepared for an opportunity takes some intelligence and some recognition of what an opportunity looks like.

Very few of us make pragmatic decisions. Most decisions are made on impulse, seeing an opportunity and seizing it. From the time Goldie was a little girl on Big Creek at the bridge until she died in the nursing home at Rogers, Arkansas, her life was lived searching for solutions to problems. The move to Bratton was to get out on her own with Dad and live as a family unit rather than being part of the plan living under the influence of Grandpa Sutterfield.

Mom didn't believe that Dad was ready to work a farm and support a family without having other members of the family around. He was always accompanied by somebody regardless of the chore he was doing. Mom taught me that the most important thing in life was to be able to be by yourself, entertain yourself, and do a job by yourself. She used the time after Nell started to school to teach me independence.

When I was with her at the nursing home and we visited for the last time, she spent her time reinforcing how being happy all of her life had depended more on her than the people she had around her. She truly believed in independence and being able to make your own decisions. She understood the need to be independent better than anybody I ever knew. While it's important to independent of other people's ideas and needs for help, it is also important to understand when you need to cooperate and ask for assistance.

She enforced the idea to me that I didn't have to know everything, that it was more important to know who to ask for information when you need it. That has been my life plan, to always know where to go for the help I need. If it's a technical problem involving a particular piece of equipment, Goldie always said, "Two kinds of people will work on a watch. One is a jeweler capable of repairing it. The other is more immediate and that is it's going to be without a timepiece."

In this digital age Goldie would have survived really well. I try to follow her rules and not tinker with anything I'm not capable of fixing. She would have loved Google. I catch myself relying on the internet to the point that I believe I'm becoming handicapped by it. I realized how much the world had changed when I was in Walmart and they had a power failure. When the power came back on the registers were down. We stood there in the store waiting for quite some time. Then they just asked us to leave. Over the public address system they said they would not be able to check anyone out until the computers came back online.

I would have loved for her to have been present that night. Her opinion would have been voiced rather loudly with quite a bit of frustration at having to leave without the items she had come to buy. I find myself a lot of times behaving like I believe she would have. This Facebook generation would have brought out the worst and the best in Goldie.

A couple of years ago I reacted like I believe she would have under the circumstances. I don't handle criticism very well at times. And I went through a period that I let several friends on Facebook get under my skin. I blocked practically everybody who had made a derogatory remark about anybody and anyone who was arrogant or antagonistic. Needless to say, I blocked some people that have chosen to not ever be friends with me again. It's hard to read an insult that you know the person writing it would never have the nerve to say it in your presence.

Under Goldie's rules, you would never let a falsehood go unchallenged. I cannot imagine how she would have dealt with this age of misinformation. I'm writing this in March of 2022. The Russian invasion of Ukraine is ongoing today. Under Goldie's rules we would "scorch that guy's britches and he would shut his mouth and take his troops and go home." I don't think the world would survive under Goldie's rules. We would probably have a nuclear war.

I haven't yet told the story about the time we lived on Bratton when a family member decided to tell a lie about my mother. I've laughed a lot about it over the years. I remember Dad being embarrassed while I sat by Mom on the tailgate of the pickup truck waiting for that person to show up at Firestone's grocery. I was five years old.

"I'm going to kick her ass until her nose bleeds," Mom said.

I can't remember if there was an actual fight, but I remember begging her to leave.

Mom lived 87 years. As I tried to recall and record her interaction in each period of time, I've had to look at the Big Creek bridge and where she was born and lived until she was in her thirties. I looked at the six years she lived on Bratton as a period of time that seems extremely long, but in reality it was rather short.

When we moved to the road to get electricity and have a school bus come by was equally short. I only lived there a total of twelve years. Mom continued to live there for years after I graduated from high school.

The next period of time in her life was her second marriage after Dad's passing. And then the longest period of time in my memories of dealing with her was the seventeen years she lived alone, and then in assisted living, and eventually in the nursing home.

When I visited her the last week she was alive she had adjusted her goals to fit her situation. She was pleased if she was able to eat her meals, go for her dialysis, interact with her roommate, and talk to us on her phone.

All of these periods of time required adjustment. During the time that she lived in Marshall, and I lived there as well, was probably the most meaningful to me. I remember Goldie's reflections on people she had in each period of her life. I see a mirror of my own opinions reflected in the ideas I learned from her.

It's impossible to evaluate people fairly. I am the worst at properly assessing someone in the beginning of a relationship, whether in business or in friends. Mark Twain wrote, "We will only live long enough to have one good dog and one good friend." I use that saying quite a lot. And I used to say it a lot to Goldie, and we would laugh about the reasons I'd said it. She taught me that relationships that could not be maintained were better off ended as quickly as possible.

There is an episode of the Andy Griffith show where Barney said, "Nip it in the bud." That can be incorporated in with Goldie's rules. She believed anything that could be a hindrance you are better off to stop it as quickly as possible. She lived that rule in her everyday life, shown by the time Jim and I stopped by her house one Saturday morning and she met us at the door with, "Don't come a step further, we're getting ready to leave and I don't have time to even talk to you." And she turned around and went back into the house. We left.

I am 77 years old. Pat and I are trying to be realistic about what we can and cannot do at our age. Goldie's rules taught me that we are to push it as hard as we can to do everything we can physically, and to work as hard as we can at the jobs we are still able to perform.

I gave Goldie's garden hoe to Sherri. Mom used that hoe as long as she was able to plant flowers. She had used it in her vegetable garden for years. Then as she got older she was limited to a little patch of flowers that she planted every spring. This was just at the end of the mobile home where she had lived by herself the last few years. She gave the hoe to Pat's mother who lived a few blocks from her, and told her she was unable to use it anymore.

Pat's mom gave it to me when she decided she wasn't able to work in the dirt with the hoe. I bought a new one when I gave Mom's to Sherri just because I'm not ready to quit digging. But I wanted the heritage tool passed on in the family.

This story of the tool and working in the vegetable garden is about determination. The one thing that keeps us going is being determined to survive. Goldie lived all of her life believing that regardless of circumstance she had to make the best of it to survive. Life was never about money. Life was about circumstances. Life was not about catering to every need of everybody she knew. Life was about keeping things in perspective.

She told me during the last few months that we visited, "The things you're aggravated about today, chances are you won't even remember them in six months." I have found this to be true. She always said, "We remember the things we choose to, and we do our best to forget the things we want to."

She also cautioned about how we remember things. "There is no bigger liar than the memory that dwells in most people's heads." That's a tough rule to digest. Embellishment is not embellishment until it's intentional. A positive person is prone to exaggerate in an exaggerated Superman-type memory. A negative person is prone to criticize and try to reduce the size and effect of something that's been accomplished.

Goldie's rules always require that you first review the facts. Things that can be proven from pictures and records that have been filed for legal purposes, these are good facts. Hearsay is tainted. Goldie always said "they say" is the biggest liar in the community. According to her there was a lot of good in almost everybody, and there was an equal amount of bad in the same people.

She upset one of her grandchildren shortly after the death of his father when she said, "He was a good guy, but everybody's got their faults and he had his, too." That young man is one of the finest members of my family, and Mom loved him dearly. After she hurt his feelings, she hurt him more by trying to explain what she said and why.

I do that same thing. I say things that are impossible to correct.

CHAPTER 9

-3•6-

Over the years Mom and I had a lot of discussions about the period of time when we all realize our lives are almost over. As I reminisced with her just before she died, she was obsessed with talking about the hereafter. Since Dad had been a minister the discussion was part of his evangelistic efforts. The idea of accepting Christ and becoming a Christian was always presented in two perspectives. One was the avoidance of punishment and going to hell, while the other was the glorious prospect of living an eternal life in heaven.

We discussed who, when, and what would be in eternity. She had been married to and lived with Dad for 38 years. After that she had been married to Radus Drewry. She had enjoyed the years she was married to Radus better than the time she spent with my dad. Goldie's rules required being honest with yourself. Shakespeare said, "To thine own self be true." That could be included as one of her rules.

She gave us a reason for her enjoyment of the time period of her second marriage. They had an absolute common interest in almost everything they did. She didn't have the pressure of raising children. She could take Sherri fishing and then drop her off at home. All the things that Pat and I enjoy about our grandchildren she enjoyed about hers. No pressure to make a living and support children. It was just a time of doing the things she wanted to do like gardening, cooking, visiting with whomever she pleased.

I can see what she meant. But, truthfully, it hurt my feelings to think she was unhappy with Dad. When I asked her about it, she laughed and said, "Oh no, that wasn't what I meant at all." She said it was just two different periods of time and you couldn't actually compare the two.

I realize now that I am about the age she was when we had this conversation what she meant. Life has always been great. In anybody's lifetime passes and we fail to realize until years later how great that particular period of time was. I understand now what she meant.

As the conversation turned to the eternities of time, and trying to answer the questions of how it would be in heaven, she reminded me that when Paul wrote about heaven there were things he saw that he could not utter, and we would never know what eternity would be like until we got there.

She did not believe in families being a unit in eternity. As a result of my conversations with her I do not, either. She always said, "It won't work. My grandfather knew me as a little girl, I knew him as an old man. You've always known me as your mother." Her main point was that age cannot exist in eternity. When Christ explained it he clearly stated there would not be marriage, nor would there be male and female.

We had this discussion early when I was a boy. It continued to be one of our favorite topics all of my life. Dad would not participate in that discussion. He said it was a hindrance to the ideas that had been practiced for so many years among Christian people.

As I got old enough to read and research the history of churches and looked at the periods of time when different ideas were developed, I came to a conclusion. Eternity has always been an impossible concept for us to understand. Temporal matters are opposed to eternal matters. One is physical while the other is spiritual. Goldie's rules believed in the concept of leaving anything alone and out of the discussion unless you had proof. I thought about that after she passed, and I tried to resolve in my mind that when we had these discussions she was saying, "So long. I have enjoyed having you as my son and I appreciate the way we have gotten along, but I have no idea what it will be like in eternity."

I'm not sure it's useful for me to have written this for anyone to read. The ideas Mom and I discussed are in conflict with all the hopes and songs and the things we hear people express after they lose somebody. There are too many unsolvable physical questions to think that relationships here on earth can continue in an eternity setting. The age we know somebody in this life and their physical conditions will not be a part of eternal conditions. It does not disturb me at all that these questions can't be answered.

Mom believed that when Paul wrote that "we would know as we are known" it meant we would have full knowledge and understanding in eternity, and did not mean we would physically recognize and know people from our lives here on earth. I have agreed with that all my life. I have taught Sunday school class, Bible study, and participated in church conversations all of my life. I have never tried to get into this discussion with any Bible study group.

Goldie's ideas that I absorbed from her, and expounded on myself, are in total conflict with the things I see on Facebook today. I don't think it's possible for people's faith in this to be sustained if they become pragmatic about how eternity is going to be. She was not bothered with the idea that her days were coming to an end from a spiritual standpoint. She trusted that it is as the Jews believe and our soul would just return to God from whence it came, and she would be absolutely gloriously pleased if that's the way it is. She believed that if God chose to work out all of those details of being a family again that it would be just fine. She believed He was capable of not upsetting a family if there was one member that failed to make it.

That paragraph has more questions than I am capable of answering, and Goldie's rules were that if you could not answer a question logically, don't ask.

I don't actually remember the last time I talked to Mom. I know we didn't end our relationship on a bad note. My memories will always be precious whether it was digging worms and going fishing or helping her cook something in the kitchen. I will always remember when she started to cook doughnuts she would say, "Sammy get in here. I want you to eat all these you want while I'm cooking because I don't want you bothering them when I'm finished." You could never beat a deal like that. I was invited to eat the best doughnuts ever made by the best cook that cooked any. Just my opinion.

Whether I will recognize her in eternity does not matter. My entire life was set in order by her, and even now she has been constantly in control of most things I've ever done.

Goldie's rules and living under Goldie's rules. They are one and the same for ever and ever and ever.

ABOUT THE AUTHOR

Sam Pemberton was born on Bratton Creek, at an old homestead that hadn't changed much since the pioneer days. The year was 1944. Pemberton graduated from Big Flat high school. After their graduation in 1962, Sam married the love of his life, Patricia Treat.

He has worked construction in the drywall trade for most of his life. Sam presently lives in the beautiful Ozarks and continues in construction, as well as developing a new adventure called The Gathering Place in Big Flat, Arkansas, which is a restoration of the old building that is referred to in the novel as the store. He hopes you'll stop by sometime.

GOLDIE'S RECIPES

Goldie's Donuts

Ingredients

1 pkg yeast
1 cup lukewarm water
1 cup milk
¼ to 1/3 cup Crisco (shortening)
1 tbsp salt
¼ cup sugar
Flour as needed

Directions

Dissolve yeast in water.
Warm milk, shortening, salt, and sugar on burner until salt and sugar are dissolved. Pour in yeast water.
Stir in enough flour to make a stiff dough. Set in refrigerator covered with a wet cloth.
When ready to make, let sit out for 15 minutes.
Place on floured board and roll out ¾ inches thick.
Using a donut cutter cut donut and hole, let rise on floured board until doubled in size.
Drop in hot oil and fry.

Icing

Sift powdered sugar and a little cinnamon.
Add hot strong coffee until thick enough to dip.

Goldie's Chocolate Rolls

As taught to me as a child
(for anyone who is used to exact measurements, this may be a challenge)

Ingredients: flour, shortening, salt, milk, cocoa,
    sugar, canola oil and butter

Preheat the oven to 350°

Directions:
    Fill a mixing bowl to the desired level with flour. Salt to taste.
    Blend shortening into the flour. A larger amount of shortening makes the crust more tender.
    Add milk and stir in until batter is smooth.
    Place the dough on a cookie sheet or other flat surface.
    Knead the dough, adding flour until the desired consistency is achieved.

    Roll the dough into a large roll approximately 2 ½ inches in diameter.
    Slice off pieces of roll large enough to roll out into thin crusts.

    Make a mixture of cocoa and sugar to suit your taste.
    Each roll should get at least three tablespoonfuls of this mixture spread in the center.
    Add chunks of butter, at least three teaspoonfuls, on top of the chocolate mixture.

Roll up each side, tucking in the ends.

Place on a liberally greased pan.

Baste the tops of the rolls with canola oil, and sprinkle with sugar.

Place in the oven for approximately 45 minutes.

(And now you'll find out if you've got a chance of being a real Hickory Hollow hillbilly chocolate roll maker!)